T0121946

Alpha State Writings

LLOYAL HIGH CLOUD WALKER

BALBOA
PRESS

A DIVISION OF HAY HOUSE

Balboa Press books may be ordered through booksellers or by contacting:

Balboa Press
A Division of Hay House
1663 Liberty Drive
Bloomington, IN 47403
www.balboapress.com
1 (877) 407-4847

Because of the dynamic nature of the Internet, any web addresses or
links contained in this book may have changed since publication and
may no longer be valid. The views expressed in this work are solely those
of the author and do not necessarily reflect the views of the publisher,
and the publisher hereby disclaims any responsibility for them.

The author of this book does not dispense medical advice or prescribe the use
of any technique as a form of treatment for physical, emotional, or medical
problems without the advice of a physician, either directly or indirectly. The
intent of the author is only to offer information of a general nature to help
you in your quest for emotional and spiritual well-being. In the event you use
any of the information in this book for yourself, which is your constitutional
right, the author and the publisher assume no responsibility for your actions.

Any people depicted in stock imagery provided by Thinkstock are
models, and such images are being used for illustrative purposes only.
Certain stock imagery © Thinkstock.

Printed in the United States of America.

ISBN: 978-1-4525-1534-2 (sc)
ISBN: 978-1-4525-1536-6 (hc)
ISBN: 978-1-4525-1535-9 (e)

Library of Congress Control Number: 2014909418

Balboa Press rev. date: 09/17/2014

Introduction

This book is intended as a strong invitation for you, the reader, to enjoy thinking outside the confines of collective consciousness.

Please be sure to read The **Hi, God Story** and **High Cloud's I Am** so that later writings will make more sense.

Enjoy!

Acknowledgments

Special thanks to Eric Flickwer

For the cover art, *Meditation,* and the

I Am artwork;

To Christina Backlund for *Moondancer,*

And to Cece Skye Walker for
Winter Whisked Away

Contents

Section Two: Pretty, Useful Stuff in Life

Prelude:

HIGH CLOUD'S NAME

"It's something about being in or walking in a high-altitude cloud. Walks in high clouds maybe" I said to Myrtha. Myrtha is a wise woman of Navajo heritage I met when I lived in Tujunga, California, and I was telling her of my vision quest back in 1991.

"The first time I saw Mount Shasta, I was on a road trip to Canada from Los Angeles in mid-September, and was driving north through Corning in northern California. Shasta was so beautiful that it brought tears to my eyes, seeing it that first time. You can feel its being from that far away, and farther; Shasta seems like a person, a long lost beloved friend you are seeing again.

"From there it was like one motion. I drove straight to Mount Shasta City, about 120 miles farther, and went in a grocery store there, where I bought three pounds of trail mix, a couple gallons of water, and a few other supplies. Then I got in my car and headed up the mountain. The road ended in a small parking lot at about 8,000 feet, so I parked my car. I loaded up my backpack, literally throwing the stuff from my suitcase into it, along with the supplies from the store. I put on my hiking shoes and headed uphill. It was tiring walking uphill at that altitude, but I felt like I was receiving energy from Shasta and I got a sense that if I just listened to Shasta and paid attention, I'd be fine. Shasta would help me and keep me safe. I looked at the ground and ahead of me, noticing the arrow-shaped rocks or branches of trees that told me which paths to take. Soon I smelled fresh water ahead and suddenly, I felt less tired. The water was like magic. I hadn't even gotten to it and it was rejuvenating me already!

"When I got to the spot where the spring came out, I must have drunk half a gallon of it. That water is INCREDIBLY GOOD! I dumped out my water bottles and refilled them from the magic stream. I was no longer the least bit tired, so I headed uphill again for a couple more hours, until it started getting dark, and I saw a reason to stop. At this altitude of around 10,000 feet the pine and fir trees had petered out to small ones, only about three or four feet tall and gnarly looking. Nearby stood two old cinder-block buildings, about nine feet square and eight feet tall. There was still some grass on the ground on the flattish area around them, but I could see that farther up the slope, the snow still hadn't melted, even this late in summer. *Ok, this is the place to spend the night,* I thought. Having some uncertainty about large predators, I decided to climb on top of the building on the right. The sun began to sink over the horizon, and the air got cold very quickly. Over my walking shorts went long pants; over the t-shirt went a long sleeve shirt, then another t-shirt; more walking shorts outside my long pants; another pair of socks, then back on with the shoes. *Ok, I'll be warm enough now,* I thought. I lay down, to sleep, I hoped. Nope! Some wind and getting still colder convinced me to climb down and go into the other building with the door.

"Now I was definitely warmer, but I had to put a slab of plywood I found there, underneath me to keep the cold concrete floor from sucking away my body heat. It worked, so I rested as best I could at that altitude, with my lungs working hard, and eventually got to sleep.

"I woke at what must have been 3:00 a.m., and through the crack in the doorway caught sight of the crescent moon going down over the horizon. When the moon went down the wind came up to an ominous whistle, reminding me how glad I was to be inside. I wedged the door closed better and rested half asleep till the sun came up, illuminating the room a little and calming the wind. I removed my extra layers, back to walking shorts, t-shirt, etc. I had some trail mix, drank that wonderful water, and was ready to go. *THAT path—yeah THAT one,* Shasta was saying to me in Shasta's Tongue. So I walked up the path along the top of a ridge for a while. Then I saw a tent on the left a little way down the slope from the ridge. The two guys there said they lived in Colorado, at about six thousand feet elevation. They were staying at that altitude for a day or two to get acclimated so they could make it to the top. That didn't worry me, I had Shasta's help for my energy and wanted to get to wherever it was I was going.

"Soon the trees all petered out, giving way to some mostly purple flowers, growing in a ring about four feet wide around Shasta at that altitude for as far as I could see. Then it was red flowers—smaller these, with bees swarming around them, in a ring all around Shasta the same way. Now yellow, smaller yet and with different shapes, going a good way up. The patches of permanent snow on the sides were getting more frequent and bigger as I ascended, and the vegetation died out to just lichen growing on the gray, sometimes crumbly rock. The air had grown very thin by now. I had started the day walking and climbing, taking rests every few minutes and doing martial arts rejuvenative breathing. Now I was using martial-arts breathing all the time and taking breaks every hundred steps, then fifty, twenty, ten, five. It got to one step for a while, then I saw ahead of me a flattened, widened area of the path where someone had put rocks in an oval and cleared a nice smooth, flat, space. I went and laid on my back in the oval with my head more uphill. Tiny transparent worms and things swam in my vision. Boy, I was glad to be laying down resting! As I lay there, Shasta's energy slowly seeped into me, reviving me, and as it did so the air around and above me gradually drew my attention. The air was wispy, thinly cloudy, and it came to me that I was within a cloud, there on Shasta. After a few long moments more, amazement struck me. *I was in a cirrus cloud*, a high-altitude cloud normally found above twenty thousand feet! Holy cow! I had walked up into a high altitude cloud! At this point I got the impression (from Shasta mostly) that I had done what I came there to do. Knowingly or not, I had completed a vision quest.

"Again filled with new energy, I stood and looked up the path, and to my disappointment, saw not far ahead, a glacier between me and the summit. That was definitely beyond what my lack of equipment allowed, not to mention my not being acclimated, or in physical condition at that point, to do that climb. *It's okay you've done remarkably well*, came the thought, with a comforting feeling, like a pat on the back, or a parents embrace. I turned, and with what seemed hardly any effort, returned down Shasta's side to my car in under three hours! I repacked my car and resumed my trip, stopping at a restaurant for some solid food on the way out. Darned if before I ate, I didn't need to use the restroom too. I hadn't had to even think about that on Shasta."

I knew that in many Native American traditions, I now had a name. The name never seemed to materialize solidly for me, though I knew it was something about being in or walking in high altitude clouds. This was why I was talking to Myrtha, she could help.

Myrtha looked at me and said, "Don't make it complicated. It's easy. You have a good name already, Lloyal Walker. Just put High Cloud in the middle, it goes right together. *Lloyal High Cloud Walker.* It suits you. You are lucky, it's a great name!"

Somewhat overcome with emotion, I said "Thank you, Myrtha. You have just named me." At this point realizing I couldn't just name myself, no matter what I had done. That's why it wouldn't gel before. I needed someone, a wise person, to name me.

Section One:
COMING FROM SOURCE

The "Hi, God" Story

One day,

God imagined himself to be
a single human being.

Why, it must be you!

Hello again, God.

High Cloud's "I AM"

In the vast unformed ocean of limitless creative consciousness which some say is the substance of God; There was no time. One instantaneous second was forever. Forever was one instantaneous second... There was no space. All the vast Universe was a dimensionless point. A dimensionless point was the vast Universe...

There was no matter. The incalculable weight of the combined galaxies of the multiple universes was a mere thought. A mere thought was the incalculable combined weight of the galaxies of all the multiple universes...

There was no energy. The incredible outpouring of all the many Universes' suns exploding with atomic fire was a fleeting thought. A fleeting thought was the out pouring of all the many Universes suns exploding with atomic fire...

A thought... The thought took form . The form was.... I AM. And the I AM thought.

The I AM thought "I AM"... and the "I AM's" thought "I AM", and the I AM was many. There was difference between the I AM'S, and thus came about distinction. And with the creation of distinction, came the basis for the idea of space. And they persisted. Thus came the basis for the creation of time. The I AM'S were getting good at this creating.

Taking stock of what has happened so far, we now have many beings, formed from limitless creative consciousness into distinct self-aware individuals. Sufficient unto themselves, in the image of what some call God, able to replicate themselves, and to limitlessly create. We have the beginnings of what we now call time and space, created by naive beings who have no insights as yet into their own nature but about to embark on an adventure.....

The I AM's pondered .....

What is an I any way? some thought. Some wondered "What is AM ?" Another wondered "What am I Here for ?" Another thought What AM I?"

Since the idea of answers hadn't even been created yet, none were forthcoming....

One I Am thought "there must be more than this!", and lo and behold, there was.(I couldn't at this point tell you what it was, but there was definitely something.)

Soon, many of the I Am's Were thinking "Why there MUST BE MORE to it than this.... Is this all there is ???" NO!!! We (Oops...was it really us?) agreed, and, OMIGAWD!! (Or maybe I should say, "Oh my biggest possible I Am !! ") The Universe exploded into Creation, scintillating, coruscating, pinwheeling, cavorting, seemingly creating itself, (with our help in reality, though we might deny it sometimes) in endless variation, for our ever continuing amusement and learning.

More later... Much more.

Love, Rev Lloyal High Cloud Walker

To those who will no doubt ask "What more?" I simply say, "CREATE IT"

God's Voice

One day I reached out
To touch the face of God.
I called out
To hear his voice.
But he fooled me.
From the highest plane,
He looked at me
With my face.
He spoke to me
In my voice.
Alas, I thought it was just me
Til' one day
It dawned on me …
What better face and eyes
To see me with,
What better voice and tongue
To speak to me in,
Than my own.

Many Faceted Faces

Source is the one who,
When you call to him
In your finite voice,
Looks instantly back
With the one facet, large or small,
Of his many, many faceted faces,
That is you,
In instant recognition
Like a long-lost loved one's embrace
And says to you
In your own mental voice
That obvious thing
You somehow couldn't get,
But had to know.

Source of All, Within Us

When I was a youth of fourteen or so in Michigan, I had a deep religious experience. My father and I, on a fall day, took the canoe out on the river. We were wearing heavy coats and big rubber boots. We put flotation cushions on the cold aluminum seats. We paddled downstream to a place in the river where there were rocks, mostly just under the surface, set there to divert water around the water treatment plant nearby.

There was a good spot about three or four feet wide where, if you kept the canoe straight, you could go right through. We started to do just that, but didn't get it quite right, and the canoe caught on a rock, sending us toppling over into the icy water. Dad and I got the canoe to the shore with all of our stuff except a floatation cushion, which was floating away.

I ran along the bank, cold and wet like my father, to go get the cushion. A little farther downstream, since I was already wet, I waded into the stream towards the middle to go get it before the river took it too far. As I waded in, the bottom suddenly dropped off, plunging me again into the icy water, with my heavy coat and rubber boots pulling me down as I tried to swim in the now frightening current.

I could feel my strength rapidly waning and was about to go under when in my head I called out to God to help me. From my heart, and the heart of every cell of my being, a new energy surged. My life force, the inspiration from source within, welled up and infused me with new strength.

I saw the cushion only a few feet from me, and with new strength swam to it, pulling my rubber boots, sodden coat, clothes and all, along. I took it and floated, swimming safely to shore, and answering my dad very tiredly, but loud enough, when he *very* worriedly called me, from some distance upstream now.

I went back with the cushion but only one boot, I had kicked the other off in the struggle, better it than me, and the river had still gotten its payment for our mistake. At the time, I thought, *Wow! There really is a God.*

I didn't realize 'til many years later that God (Goddess if you're a woman) is the wellspring of our life force within us, manifesting in our lives and our very existence. He manifests through our sanity and inner strength, giving us life as his children, to mirror all human aspects of himself through our lives.

The concept of being "the one true god" is limiting to that being. God, as the All and the All within us, cares not for the separation of numbers categorizing our separation from him and one another.

I experience God as the Source beyond counting, while being all that is, including myself.

A Reverent Purpose

The main purpose in being a reverend
Is NOT to be revered,
But to inspire realizations
About spirituality
In people
And their relationships
With themselves
As Source.

God's Evolution

Self-awareness is the key to the evolution
Of mankind
And the evolution
Of God himself
Since he needs us
As his eyes, ears, and,
Differing from his,
Viewpoint.
In God's image, we evolve ourselves
Through our awareness, and so he

Likewise mirrors us,
And out of the unformed
creative consciousness
Comes the formation of God himself:
More evolved.*

* An excellent measure of sentient evolution
is a beings ability to encompass, without
judgement, multiple and varying viewpoints.

God's Favorite

When we each and every one
of us formed ourselves and
Our Universe out of the limitless sea of
Consciousness, which is
the essence of God,
We each and every one of
us had to decide
Which self, in this or any other Universe,
To be.
Naturally, each and every one of us
Chose the best possible self in
the universe to become.
That's why each and every one of us is
God's favorite
Child.

Qualms of God

God has no qualms
About each and every one of us
Having the experience of being him.
He considers that we are able to
At will anyway
Whether we need to rediscover that
Or not.

Working Hands

We are the hands of Source, working.
We are the voice of Source, speaking.
We are the mind of Source, reasoning.
We are the heart of Source, loving.
We are the will of Source, Creating.

Feeling Godlike

As the me that exists in the finite,
To the me that lives as the infinite pool
Of creative consciousness, I can
Always deny myself to myself,
Thereby frustrating myself.
Or maybe I could just reach
on up to that light
And have that me give me
more of myself from there.
After all, I don't miss it there,
Being infinite and all.
And I could use a lot more of that me
Down here, it makes me
Feel
Almost
Godlike.

Mile in My Shoes

I heard it through the grapevine
That Source will walk
A mile in my shoes one day.
But I don't know which day,
And I don't want to ruin it for him …
So I guess I'll just have to
Make every day my best.

The Sparkle

Our Individuality and free will
Has, to Source observing it,
The value of the sparkle in the eyes
Of the one we love most,
When we see that it is there
Because it's mutual.

The Anointed One

An anointed one wanted to be human for a while. The weight of the world's sins on his shoulders was just wrong. Whenever he incarnated and tried to teach people about their own godhead, they killed that incarnation of him. He couldn't use that identity afterward either. The people would be guilty and remorseful and put weird psychic energy lines into him. It tired him. They kept getting him to heal them, but they refused to stay healed.

So he rejected his old identities, deciding to be a warrior. He got shot down over France. So he became a commando next time. Another commando executed him; high command thought he knew too much.

Okay, he'd go to America, away from the wars, and be a metal smith. It was a pretty good life, but he never fit in well with the other humans. They couldn't remember their past incarnations for one thing, and they thought in short term because of it. He wasn't going to forget his past if he could help it. Just to fit in? *NO WAY!* It was a nice life anyway though. A few decades in however, he couldn't deny his own nature. It was getting to be a decently long life and it was the information age. People were actually accepting him now. He didn't always talk about metalsmithing and the weather just to get along. He could actually speak about the nature of mankind and God with people. No one tried to kill him and it was fun. Some were learning from him, and most refreshingly, he was learning from them!

One day he had a big upset though. Someone told him about a spiritual group she was in and how wonderful it was. At the meeting members divulged who they invoked when they engaged in a healing. With the majority of the group it was one of his old incarnations! Thousands of years later! He knew from memory that he had always wanted people to invoke God within themselves. He still wanted them to, it was his nature. And he knew God wanted them to also. Imagine invoking another man for healing power. "Oh great Kavorkyan, bless my healing and give it sacred energy." *Give me a break, please*! He thought. He asked them why they didn't invoke the source, the infinite one, first creator of all. They said that it was the same thing. The anointed one was crestfallen. Would even the more enlightened ones not learn? *They were all incarnations of infinite source and could invoke infinite source! How could they try to give that away to someone who didn't even want to be anything but human anymore?* What were they thinking?

He went home and asked God. "Why am I trying to enlighten these people? They are unbelievable. They say they know they are incarnations of your essence and they not only don't invoke Godhead but instead invoke somebody who never even existed as the image they have of him." God patiently replied, *"I can see this is a game that is not at all fun for you, but if it were too easy and not a challenge, you would not have wanted the game."* The anointed one laughed uproariously until he cried, and he felt better. When the anointed one told me this story, I laughed until I cried and I felt better too.

Section Two:
PRETTY, USEFUL STUFF
IN LIFE

Breath of Morning Meditation

Waking freshly in your
bright morning calm,
Breathe in the freshness,
The warm, yet cool, glow
Of the white-gold life light,
Pouring, streaming down,
Floating in trillions of molecule sized
Bits that vivify you,
From lungs outward,
Expanding your consciousness,
Your *prana*, your *chi*.
Let it take you to that ecstatic place

Where no symbols exist, and feel the all,
Conceptualizing it in wordless,
Blissful acceptance.
Breathe the breath out
now, letting it carry
The product of your living out
into the world with it,
Your will, the impetus of
your hearts desires,
For the universe to receive
and be shaped by.
Continue in a cycle of universal breath
And life that will shape positively
In an upward spiral, this
life and all it touches.

Moondance

Full moon on silvery, shimmering
Satiny spirit skin, we dance
Through and above the clouds, we dance
Bodies asleep at home in bed, we dance
Attached by shiny silvery
threads, we dance
Through our shadowy sleeping
dreams, we dance
For joy of life, still to live, we dance
Until the morning's call to wake
And some slim glimmerings
Of that joy we take
Out into the world we send
The dance of joy that has no end

Life's Meaning

Anything in this world
Including life itself
Has to you only the meaning
That you yourself,
By your first act of creation,
Create and assign to it.
Make it useful,
Profound, and happy
And so will your life be.

Real Progress

Okay, so the meaning of life is
what you create it to be.
It distills down further to life's purpose,
To create.
The question then arises, create what?
In general, it seems
More and better life.
On a personal level, the
successful creation of self,
Continually improving, is evolution.
You've got to create yourself
continuously anyway,
Better to evolve.
On other levels change is also
inevitable. Do your best
To take control and evolve
things there too,
Moving all toward better life.
I would call that true progress!

Are You Sure?

It's about certainty.
Certainty is what brings
effectiveness to our assertions.
In some religions they call it faith.
One religion even has the concept
hidden in plain sight,
Defining its name as "Knowing
how to know".
More literally, it means the
study of how to know,
Or the study of the subject
of knowledge itself.
For most people, to *know*
something is to have
Complete understanding and
certainty of its existence,

Through whatever it takes to achieve that.
Some crave the word of
an authority figure.
Others need a PhD, still others
nothing more than a ritual.
Faith, on the other hand,
Doesn't require understanding
or experience; only belief,
That might not match reality.
On a large scale, numbers
of people believing
Can create and change realities.
This phenomenon can be and
is harnessed by religion,
As religious leaders instinctively know.

Those who reject the faith or
refuse the blind belief
Are reviled, excommunicated, killed,
as heretics, infidels, suppressive,
And unbelievers. With good reason.
Realities created by belief without
factual understanding to solidify them
Usually implode when
doubt is introduced.
That doubt destroys a religious
leader's ability to control his flock.
Imagine if everyone knew
what it meant to be
An autonomous extension
of the ultimate creator.

Consciousness Endures

I am immortal.
I have always been.
I always will be
I change, often imperceptibly slowly,
Sometimes blindingly fast,
Enough to disorient.
And my consciousness
tenaciously endures.

Breath of Creation

Out past Saturn where the
formlessness is pure,
I breathe in the fresh void,
craving to form.
I pause, then exhale creations
beyond counting,
Blissfully joyful, to exist.

Old Shadows

Always create your own reality,
For if you don't,
Old shadows and others
Will create it for you,
And
Can you trust them
To know what you want,
Or to care?

Out of Mass Consciousness

That thing which the collective
Consciousness believes cannot be
Changed, will *appear* to be immutable
Reality for any individual associated with
That reality.
An escape from this
Is to disassociate from the mass
consciousness reality thus created,
By changing one's viewpoint,
proximity to it,

Energy level, wavelength, job category,
And so on. One may
become less visible to
Others sharing the reality in
this way, which often can
Cause a loss of interaction
for the individual
Not buying into the immutability,
reality, or the belief creating it.
Mass consciousness will
Evolve as individuals within it evolve,
Yielding an evolved shared reality.

For Those Who Pass On the Knowledge

I've always thought that the best
gift you can ever give someone
Is more of himself.
To pass on knowledge and skills
that give people the ability
To do what they want to
do, or do it better,
Has got to be one of the highest
Purposes in this Universe.
If one considers that God is omnipotent,
And omniscient,

Then moving mankind, even one person,
Even a little bit,
In that direction must be a holy act.
Hats off to those who take it on as a job,
And to all who do it regularly,
A heartfelt thanks from all of us,
Maybe even from God too,
Who benefit from it.
Thank You.

Spirit Touch

The gentle loving touch
Of a still-living (but bodiless) spirit
Upon my warm skin
Reminds me that
Our reach extends far beyond
The realms we see and hear
To places that we think
Are only imagined.

Will Tuning

When two or more are gathered
in the One's name,
The One's will will be done.
Tuned in, the One's will is my will.
The will of the One energy source …
now formless, Will be my will
It is mine to shape the ONE
energy by my will,
Into forms amenable to it and me,
Which forms come effortlessly when
One, myself, or two too are tuned to it.
Stay tuned to it.

Soulless Organization

A soulless organization is defined as
An organization which uses none of the
Attributes one would think of as spiritual
In its decision-making policies.
Some of these spiritual attributes are
Fairness, honor,
Conscience, responsibility,
Accountability, and truthfulness,
As well as
Individual respect, openness,

And a strong inclination to
The greatest good for the
greatest number,
Among others. Beings with
souls working with
And fostering the agenda of organizations
Without, tend to become
As though soulless themselves.
Living robots.

Human Machinery

A machine given a heart
and soul acquires,
For better or worse,
Conscience, honor, principles,
courage, empathy,
a sense of fairness,
And generally,
A desire to effect the greatest good.

Made in Heaven on Earth

Good relationships may be created
By heavenly agreements,
But to expand them
In richness and fulfillment,
We must clear them
Of our own
Limiting beliefs.

Awareness Prayer

Negative statement:

Let me never miss awareness of anything pertinent to an activity of mine, so that it causes me or the activity to suffer, fail, become misdirected, nor cause me to hesitate longer than the appropriate delay for thought.

Positive statement:

Always let me be aware of everything pertinent to a desired activity of mine that can help me or it to succeed, and let my awareness cause me and my endeavor, as well as other desired ones connected, to succeed and win, thus pleasing myself and others.

Tractor Beam Acquisition

If you wish to retrieve something that was lost, misplaced, or stolen, this technique has been effective.

Conceive the signatory vibration of the item's essence, including things you really like or can easily have about the thing.

Envision that vibrational essence and the thing itself as a solid anchor point.

Set your front porch, parking spot, pet's food dish, or yourself up as another solid anchor point.

Hook a line—a beam—between the two points using thought energy or visualization.

Next, have the beam shorten and pull the two points together, using full power. Picture it using the energizing power of all the loose energy floating around the universe at large. That way it can stay turned on, and not give you headaches from the energy and keeping your attention on it all the time. It's a lot of energy, but it's worth it.

Get in touch with several positive friends and have them add energy and reality to the tractor beam and its results.

Go on about your business without keeping your attention on it, and be ready to receive the lost item back. Most things will find their way into your possession within just a few days.

Good Luck!

Get a Mirror

If you are looking for a savior,
Get a mirror.
Nobody can do it better
than you anyway.

Section Three:
IN LOVE, MORE
PRETTIES

The Gift

There is a precious part of us
That doesn't live, unless we give it
Very simply, unconditionally, and
With no constraint.
I love you.

Love Requited, Breathlessly Excited

Her smooth, soft, silky warm skin
And firm, gentle, loving hands
Pulling me in
Lost in flowing, gentle, herb-scented hair
Kissing sweet, nibbling lips
Wanting me deeply, gently in there
Hearts beating alike
As breath and flesh mingle
Words of love murmured
As nerve endings tingle
With a soaring crescendo
Of love requited
And just the thought
Leaves me breathlessly, excited.

To Sky With Love

When I get up in the morning and
Fill my breath with live air,
Do I say, "I love you, air?"
When I am refreshed and replenished
By a drink of clear, fresh water,
Do I say "I love you" to the water?
When I feel the warm sun on my face,
The fresh earth and grass at my feet,
And see the open sky

Stretching over my head,
Do I say,
"I love you, earth and grass
and sun and sky?"
No, of course not.
But to anyone seeing us
It is plain that
That is how I love you
And it will remain so.

Love, High Cloud

Winter, Whisked Away

'Twas the month before
Christmas and I was in L.A.,
When a big blue eyed man came
and whisked me away.
"To mountains of green
and sky of pure blue,
That's where I live and
where I'm taking you."

He came like a knight to
save me from the city;
I had to leave friends and that was a pity.
As we got farther north I
was getting his point,
And my nose was no longer
so far out of joint.

We drove in two cars
pulling trailers a-rear,
Up and down many hills,
shifting gear to gear.
I felt my heart swell and we
shared many smiles
As our journey home became
less and less miles.

We drove into the mountains,
and saw fresh snow;
My warm blood was screaming,
"Oh no! Oh no!"
When he'd left it was warm,
and he'd done what it took
To have running water to
shower and cook.

Imagine his shock at seeing
everything frozen
His water pipes were sticking out,
and yes, they were broken!
And I, as the warm country
wife, am ashamed
When I look back and see
how terribly I blamed.

Today as I write this, our
home's back together,
And my new mountain home's
having beautiful weather.
At long last my husband and I can share
The life we'd been awaiting.
What more is there?

(c) 11/26/2000 Cecelia Skye Walker *

*Printed here by special permission

Dreaming

A breast
Held against a hand cupped,
And never needing to let go.
Asleep beside one so precious,
That all time is worth this one moment,
And no wish to wake from this dream.

Sparkling Laughter

Beloved images in a waking dream
Lying still, beside her,
Touching full length our bodies,
She holds my cupped hands
Against bare breasts.
Holding hands clasped gently,
Without the thought of ever having to
Let go.
Words from an old song:
"Half of me is all of her
I am much happier,
She makes me whole."
Dancing eyes creating magic,
Sparkling laughter,
And *love*.

Section Four:
REGULAR STUFF IN ALPHA STATE

I Pilot the Whales

I pilot the many-wheeled whales of steel
From whose vast maw,
Or whose wide, flat back,
I bring the many things
To free you from lack.
Fuel, fresh food, paper, glass and steel.
These and much more, ride my
whale of many wheels.
Through high mountain tunnels,
Over plains and mighty rivers,

Snow, ice, and tire chains
Give me the shivers.
Traffic jams are rivers of molten taillights,
Man, I would love
To again see the sights
Of open road,
Sweet meadow,
Snowy mountains of white.
Ten gears, forty tons,
Curves shifting freight,
Boy, oh boy
I hope I'm not late.

They say this job is for the unskilled,
Yet if bureaucrats did it,
They would surely be killed.
Height, weight, and length,
Did I get enough sleep?
Out of the scales
The D.O.T. creeps,
Looking, always looking,
To spot something wrong,
But still somehow nowadays,
I am six million strong.

I am father, mother, son, cousin or wife
Indeed, I have come from all walks of life.
Many nights alone, I sleep in my truck,
When I see my loved ones,
I've had some good luck.
Depressed, downhearted,
tired and distraught?
No, I'll end on a much better thought,
If you have it,
By my many wheeled whale,
it was brought.

Pipe's Song

Life is good when you're on two wheels,
Accelerating up an 8 percent grade at 80.
Fresh wind in your face,
Your motor thrums
While your pipes sing
Their sweet exhaust song.
You pass a truck grinding its way up,
And the driver as you pass
Is wishin' he was doin' that
So strong *you* can feel it.
Yeah, life is definitely good.

Dimples Greeting

May you have sparkles in your eyes
Dimples on your cheeks
A smile on your face
And a song in your heart.

Iron Horses, You Say?

My mechanical carriage is not
drawn by horses, but
Produces in its machinery
the power of more than
Three hundred of them,
Enough to hurl me with it
Across a continent,
In a matter of two days or so.
I must feed it, not hay,
But distilled liquid fire,
And its waste is not stinky droppings
Left on the ground,
But mostly odorless fumes
That can kill you.

The Sun's Breath

The sun has wisdom.
He knows birth,
Life, and death,
And breathes them all
In one breath.

Whistle Song

It's the whistle song
Of power from the turbo,
As I crest another hill,
Catching yet another gear.
It's the staccato snarl of the jake brakes,
Changing rhythm, four, six, two
cylinders, as I flip the switches
For changing downhill inclines.
It's the little kids, pumping closed fists,
Forearms upright, out Dad's car window,
That make me say,
"Sometimes this job is
pretty good anyhow."

Friends on the Road

Sometimes out on the road,
When the singing of tires on pavement
Becomes a cold whine,
When the sweet burble of
the exhaust note
Starts to sound hollow,
When the vast freedom of the open road
Just looks empty,
I remember friends
Laughing over a turn of a phrase

And a smoke in the shop,
My laundry neatly folded on my bed,
After I'd left it in the dryer.
The phrase
From a mother to young daughters
"If *you* were married to him
You'd keep him."
Little girls giggling,
Saying "I love you."
A dog licking my hand
In the morning to wake me.

Remembering these things,
And my friends
Who took me into their home and hearts
For as long as I could stay,
My heart fills,
And the exhaust burbles sweetly again,
The tires sing on the road,
And the Long stretch of open highway
Welcomes me,
Like true friends do for each other
Always.

Star Valley

On a moonless night,
The San Joaquin Valley stretches out,
A dark ocean
On either side,
With islands of tiny lights
Twinkling in clusters
Many miles away,
Like little manmade galaxies
Mimicking the sky above them.

Inspired by Einstein

Problems are solved
At a higher awareness
Than where
We create them.

Spark Evolution

Spark personal spiritual evolution
In as many people as you can
Thereby improving the
collective consciousness
And this world we must all live in